UNSPOKEN

Body Language & Human Behavior for Business Success

by

Shiran Cohen

Copyright © 2021 Defining Moments Press, Inc. and Shiran Cohen

All rights reserved. No part of this book may be reproduced in any form without permission in writing from the author. Reviewers may quote brief passages in reviews.

DISCLAIMER No part of this publication may be reproduced or transmitted in any form or by any means, mechanical or electronic, including photocopying or recording, or by any information storage and retrieval system, or transmitted by email without permission in writing from the author. Neither the author nor the publisher assumes any responsibility for errors, omissions, or contrary interpretations of the subject matter herein.

Any perceived slight of any individual or organization is purely unintentional. Brand and product names are trademarks or registered trademarks of their respective owners.

Defining Moments ™ is a registered Trademark
Editing: Emily Crawford-Margison
Cover Design: Defining Moments Press, Inc

Content

Dedication 1
Introduction 3
Chapter 1. Desired Reality 11
Chapter 2. Zoom In 29
Chapter 3. 7 Steps to Hire Smarter 46
Chapter 4. Fearless Impact 67
Chapter 5. The Unspoken Leader Skills 76
Acknowledgements 86
About the Author 89

Dedication

This book is dedicated to my cousin Major Mor-Yehuda Elraz (1976 - 2002) and to my cousin Maya Elharar (1976 - 1994), who both lost their lives prematurely to violent terrorism.

Introduction

I came home and I saw my mom, my sister, and brother crying. The TV was on, and the news showed that a terror attack had occurred. Eight people were killed and 55 were injured. The terror organization Hamas claimed responsibility for the attack.

Then they told me that my cousin Maya was killed; she was only 18 years old.

It was in 1994, and I was 9 years old at the time. I had just gotten back from school.

I loved Maya so much and I wanted to go to her funeral, but my parents wouldn't allow me to go with them.

Everybody said it was total chaos.

The next day, we went to visit the family. I stepped into Maya's room, and on the table there were two small bags. In one of the bags, there were 117 nails that the doctors took out of Maya's body. In the other bag was all of Maya's jewelry that had melted from the heat of the explosion.

I was holding those bags in my hand, and I just couldn't understand why.

Growing up in Israel, the holy land, a country that had suffered from terror, has its own price, and sometimes the price is a human life. We had to protect ourselves from the very beginning, and sometimes bury our loved ones.

In 2002, my cousin Mor was killed by a terrorist. Mor was 25 years old. He was exactly the type of person that people would call a hero.

Major Mor-Yehuda Elraz served in the Israeli military. He and another soldier were killed while chasing terrorists who had killed a woman. Mor and his fellow soldier were able to stop the terrorists before they died and saved many more lives.

About 6 weeks prior, Mor had visited us. He drove for three hours late in the evening just so he could stay for a half hour and then drove all the way back.

My father had a heart attack and he passed away. Mor came to show his respect, condolences, and support. It was a very stressful time security-wise in Israel, so he couldn't stay for long.

That was the last time I saw him.

I lost two cousins in two different terror attacks. To me, body language was a necessary survival tool to keep myself and other people safe.

Living in that reality makes you cautious in your environment from a very young age. You learn to observe people's behavior, looking for danger, and to be aware of the risk. In Israel, the government requires all citizens (male and female) to serve in the military. When I served, women served for two years and men for three years after primary school. One of the key things we were taught was to pay attention to suspicious behaviour and body language.

In this book, you will learn about our communication skills, or more accurately, our non-verbal communication skills and human behavior. The knowledge in this book will provide you with understanding more of the UNSPOKEN message in your life and business.

I served two years in the Israeli military and 10 years of defense work preventing terrorism in aviation worldwide. Body language and human behavior were part of my daily job for many years.

The thing is that we are all using body language, whether we want to or not. It's an essential part of our communication skills. In fact, only 7% of our communication is represented by our words; 55% is our body language and 38% is the tone of our voice.

Those percentages are based on the research of psychologist, professor, and author Albert Mehrabian, which was presented in his book *Silent Messages* (1971).

But those are just percentages, right? people are communicating anyway, even if they don't know or don't think they understand other people's body language.

Our subconscious brain represent 80% of our minds. It determines our action, our behaviour, our fears and anxieties, and so much more. But it is also responsible for many of our daily decisions. The decision of whether you are going to like a certain person or not, If you will be willing to listen to another person or not. These decisions are 100% based on our non-verbal communication, and it only takes the brain a split second to make that decision.

If you are an entrepreneur, a business owner, a team leader, or a manager, you definitely want to stick with me in this book. The modern times that we are living in require us to transform our businesses and also the way we communicate with our employees and clients.

Would you prefer only to communicate 7% of your message, running your business communications based on partial messages? Or would you rather have an advantage just by learning some non-verbal communication skills and understanding human behavior?

Non-verbal communication is required in any situation where we are communicating with other human beings, or even animals, whether it's one-on-one, in person, standing on the stage in front of an audience, or maybe even on a Zoom call. The way we are communicating and behaving directly affects the energy and how well people receive our messages.

Lately, we've been using different technology to communicate: a camera, microphone, and screen.

Think about it for a minute.

Your employees and clients can only see a part of your body. That means that they only see a part of your non-verbal communication because most of your body is out of the frame, and this goes for them, too. It's most likely that you can't see your clients' and employees' full body language as you normally would at in-person meetings. Furthermore, you are not present in the same space as they are, so the environment is different, which can affect a person's body language.

So what is it about body language that allows us to have an advantage in business? Well, the answer is simple. As humans, our conscious actions are driven from how we feel about something or certain situations. If you are able to see how something makes a certain person feel, or if you know how to use your body language and words to affect the subconscious mind and the emotional mind, you can affect the other person's actions.

I'm using non-verbal communication skills every day, and so do you, but it's your decision how you articulate, not only with your words but also with your tone of voice and your body language.

Using the strategies in this book is a simple way to immediately improve your results in the business environment, but they can also be effective in your personal life and with how you communicate and convey messages to others.

In every situation—when I'm talking to people, when I'm having a conversation in front of a client, when I'm presenting myself in front of the camera, or whenever I'm in front of an audience—I'm using non-verbal communication skills. This skillset is even more important to know how to use in stressful situations such as job interviews, negotiations, or talking with any authority figure. These skills gave me an understanding of the UNSPOKEN in every aspect of my life.

In this book, I will talk about the most common problems that entrepreneurs ask me about:

- How can I present myself better in front of an audience or camera?
- What has changed with our communication skills lately that directly affects our businesses?
- Is body language on Zoom different?
- What should I avoid, and how can I improve my self-confidence when I'm using my body language?
- What should I pay attention to when I'm hiring someone new?
- How do I use non-verbal communication to create a positive impression on others?

- How do I deal with unwanted situations like insecurity, mistakes, or incorrect body language?
- How can we increase the probability of getting what we want by using non-verbal communication?
- How do I use the right body language when asking for money?
- How can I have the UNSPOKEN advantage while interviewing and negotiating?
- Why is effective body language crucial for success?

In each chapter, you will find action steps or exercises that you can immediately apply to your life, behavior, and non-verbal communication skills.

As you go through the steps, remember that I'll be right here to help if you get stuck. You can always reach out to me via email:

Shiranunspoken@gmail.com.

Chapter 1.
Desired Reality

In March 2013 I was injured in a severe car accident, and since then, everything has changed for me.

This was not the first trauma I had gone through in life. By that point, I already knew the meaning of physical pain—mental, spiritual, loss, and grief.

I already knew cruelty and severe violence. I already knew what it meant to feel out of control and helpless. I had already collected the fragments and put on the armor that hides the suffering and pain hundreds of times.

I was proud of my ability to move on at any cost, to get on my feet. Despite the pain and shame, I was always able to get back to routine quickly and convey a picture that everything was fine, that I was successful; an excellent student and athlete in high school, an excellent commander in the army, an outstanding employee in preventing terrorism in aviation, trophies and medals from sports, certificates, awards and prizes. This is the person everyone knew.

Pain was not new to me in 2013 when the accident happened. What was new to me was that I could not recover quickly. I could not recover from the injuries, some of which exist to this day as irreversible damage. I have CRPS (Complex Regional Pain Syndrome) in my right hand, and I am diagnosed with PTSD (Post Traumatic Stress Disorder). It was not the physical pain that prevented me from recovering but the many scars my soul had suffered during life that broke my spirit.

I lost myself, and at some point, also the desire to live.

- ✓ I am HUMAN.
- ✓ I am a SURVIVOR.
- ✓ I am a WARRIOR.
- ✓ I am a SOLDIER.
- ✓ I am a LEADER.

and I do NOT GIVE UP without a fight!

Each of us has our own life story, and each of us brings himself or herself to every interaction with other people. You have a story, your family members have a story, your customers, your employees, a bank clerk, a shop assistant, an idiot who cut you off on the road—they all have a story.

The thing that is important to understand is that you bring yourself, they bring themselves, and we all bring our stories whether we want to or not.

The meaning of this is you will never know another person as you know yourself and vice versa. That is, each of you comes to the conversation from a different perspective.

Communication is used by us in our daily lives and in our businesses. You can create the desired reality that works best for you and your business even if you are communicating through technology.

Like in any other thing in life, you must know your desirable outcome. Ask yourself:

- What message do I want to convey?
- What kind of person, manager, employer, or leader do I want to be?
- How do I want others to see me?
- How do I want others to feel in my presence?
- What do I need to change or do to get my desired result?

This book is written in a very unusual time that requires us to pivot and make a lot of changes in our life and business worldwide. Even though some of the examples in this book are addressing technology solutions for meetings, all the information can also be applied in face-to-face meetings.

Since many people are struggling with the new daily routine, I choose to give some examples from the virtual world we've been all living in recently.

1.1 - Human behavior while working from home

A large number of conversations and meetings take place in front of a computer screen and a camera. Usually, the level of attention and concentration that the participants in the conversation have is not high because they work from home, in an environment that has a lot of distractions or even the feeling of "I am at home." That is, it makes it difficult for us to concentrate and get into work mode.

We sit and work and suddenly remember that we did not wash the dishes in the sink, we have to make a groceries list, and now we also want to eat something...

Like any other person, when you are alone and no one sees what you are doing, you will usually make "discounts" for yourself. You will act and react differently with people or to people when no one else is around. This is based on the environment, relationships, your emotions, and state of mind.

Do you talk differently to your family members compared to your friends or clients?
Do you eat differently when you are alone or when you are at a restaurant?
Are there things that you're doing in private that you would never do in public?

Understand that because we behave differently when we are in front of other people, how close we are to them and how much time those people spend with us will determine the level of exposure that we will allow them to see. Everybody behaves differently when they are alone compared to when they are with other people.

So we can expect that other people will behave in different ways with different people in different environments.

When we work in an environment alone with ourselves, the energy is different; we feel less connected and belonging than in the workplace, and therefore it is easier for us to succumb to distractions.

This in no way implies that you are lazy or do not care. It just means you are human.

In such a situation, stress increases because you feel that you are not being productive enough. You worry and feel bad about yourself because you are not getting the results you want within the time frame you want.

In addition, you feel stressed by your boss who wants you to provide answers and meet goals, and now you also have a Zoom call with the boss and staff...
How do you feel? Do you want to be on that call? Probably not.

If you are the boss or the one who summoned the call, this is how your employees feel.
The way we feel will affect our decisions and, as a result, our actions and outcome.

So what can you do about it? How can you create the necessary energy and focus on your calls? Can we create a comfortable environment?

You show up as the leader to your people. The leader they need you TO BE.

We must first understand a number of basic things about human behavior.

- **What we see, hear, feel, think, and process in our thoughts is the reality from our point of view.**

Throughout life, we have created patterns based on what we are familiar with.

When you think of the word "light," do you interpret a positive or negative connotation?

What about "darkness"?

Is fear "good" or "bad"?

Is sadness "good" or "bad"?

Do you understand where I'm heading? The reality is that "good" and "bad" are not real.

Could you feel happy and differentiate the feeling from other emotions if you never knew sadness?

Is it an important survival mechanism to feel fear in certain situations that could endanger our well-being or our lives?

What is actually real is harmony and disharmony, and if the word "light" is a positive trigger for the most part, you can create lighting in your environment to add a feeling—you create harmony that will trigger positively in the other person's mind, but understanding how other people see us in reality is necessary. In fact, when we communicate with people, they do not see us as we see ourselves or as we really are.

1.2 - We can create triggers by setting up our environment to convey the right message with our non-verbal communication.

Let me describe two pictures as examples to demonstrate how the environment by itself can trigger a feeling.

Picture 1: Zoom call with your boss or a client
Your boss or client is at their home office and behind them you can see a dresser. There is a lamp that spreads a warm light, and right next to it is a picture of their children and several other decorative items that they have collected over the years.
On the side is a reclining chair, and next to that, a shelf with books.

Everything is neat and organized.

Ask yourself:
- How comfortable and relaxed you feel when you look at such an environment.
- Do you feel relatable to that person?
- Will you feel capable of having a friendly conversation?
- Do you feel threatened?
- Are you thinking, "that person is out of my league"?

Picture 2: Zoom call with your boss or a client
The person you are talking to is sitting in their home office. Behind them there is a wall full of certificates of excellence and awards.
On the back dresser is a home printer and several folders.

Everything is organized and tidy.

Ask yourself:
- How comfortable and relaxed you feel when you look at such an environment.
- Do you feel relatable to that person?
- Will you feel capable of having a friendly conversation?
- Do you feel threatened?
- Are you thinking "that person is out of my league"?

In which of the two pictures will you feel more free to be yourself?

When the environment is personal, it creates a positive trigger like "light," inviting us to feel comfortable with having a deeper conversation. We feel that we know the person in front of us personally and become less defensive.

In fact, we create in our heads the person in front of us. Do not get me wrong. I am not saying that you are having conversations with imaginary people, but we come to every interaction with people from our individual points of view. That is, we have opinions and feelings that are based on our beliefs and a whole life experience.

We judge by our standards and opinions even though we do not know for sure something specific about a particular person. We attribute to them a "category" from the warehouse of categories we have built in our heads during life.

When you look at another person's clothing, you might ask yourself, "What the hell is he wearing?" This doesn't mean that what he is wearing is wrong or ugly or shocking. In fact, this is your perspective according to your opinions and standards.

Your judgment is only an indication of your perspective, so even when someone is actually judging you it does not say anything about you and says a lot about them.

As human beings, the fear of judgment is a fear that every person experiences, and sometimes we allow this fear to take over and determine for us the course of our lives.

We will give up and not do something we want so that people won't laugh at us or say something bad about us. We don't want to fail. We sometimes give up on our dreams, our happiness, or health just so people won't judge us.

In my previous book, "*BECOME BRILLIANT - RoadMap from Fear to Courage,*" I expanded on the understanding of judgment and provided tools for how to act in spite of fear.

Search online to find the book: "Become Brilliant Shiran Cohen"

Understanding emotions and what drives human behavior will give you a huge advantage in being able to understand non-verbal communication because, in fact, non-verbal communication reveals the emotion an individual is feeling but will not tell you why they feel that way. You will need to understand based on your familiarity with human behavior and ask questions that will give you the answer to the "why."

You can directly influence how another person sees you from his perspective.

In a conversation with one of my mentors, Shane Therault, he described to me how a certain person who had just started his career as a real estate agent was able to quickly create the impression that opened the door to a successful business for him.

All he did was shoot videos and talk about selling homes while "creating a stage." But what created the success was the optical illusion. What does that mean? He filmed these videos as he walked down the driveways of houses that had a "sold" sign on the lawn.

Though he was not involved in the sales, the viewer's impression was that this person has a tremendous success with selling homes. You can probably imagine how he managed to thrive quickly in his business.

We rely on what we see as existing and real. So when we visually see something that reinforces the words being said, we get the illusion that they are true and real.

You probably know the phrase "I'll believe it when I see it."

I know you're currently thinking, "it borders on fraud" or "it's a manipulation." You are not mistaken, but there are many ways to use any piece of information or tool.

You can use your vehicle as a means of transportation or as a lethal weapon against a person. In the same way, you can create an environment according to how you want the other to see you, your personality, and expertise.

If you want to give the impression that you are a senior manager and above everyone else, the effect of certificates and awards on the wall will make most people think that you are way above the average person and that you are successful. Most people will compare themselves to others, and if they have't achieved that level of success, it will be almost impossible for them to relate to you right away. You will provide this "important manager" feeling, but you need to understand that it will also create a distance between you and the person in front of you. It will be very difficult for them not to feel like they need to impress you, and it will add stress to the conversation. Indeed, sometimes we want to create these situations.

As I mentioned earlier, I served two years in the Israeli army and directly commanded 42 soldiers. In the first months of training the soldiers, the commanders maintained a "distance," which meant that the soldiers did not know anything personal about their commanders except their names. They did not address the commanders by their names but by rank and position status ("Yes, Sergeant" or "Yes, Commander" but NEVER "Yes, Shiran").

There is rigid discipline, and any breach of discipline, even if done inadvertently, would result in punishment.

It could be anything. If a soldier forgot to button a button on their shirt, they would be punished. Most often, such a case would result in a penalty of time. On the weekend when everyone went home and left the base at 10 a.m., the soldier who got a penalty would stay an extra hour for each time they forgot to button a button in their shirt during the week. Maybe you're thinking, "it's awful." Maybe you think, "it's not too bad," but for an 18-year-old soldier who had two days off at home after a week or a month, every minute is important. Staying an hour when everyone has already left for the weekend feels like an eternity.

Being late would result in punishment in time or in physical effort. For example, every 10 seconds a soldier was late they would "pay" with 10 minutes of running. If a soldier was a minute late, they would run for an hour. (Those are just examples. It's not set in stone as military roles; the commander decides how to handle any situation as such.)

So what do you think? Does it work?

Definitely!

There are usually a few soldiers who arrive late in the first two days, but after you are punished, you make sure it does not happen again. Even if you watched it and saw someone else running, you immediately realize that no one is playing games here or will give you any leniency. The result is that everyone arrives before the set time.

Is the mentality and sense of "distance" that your commander is above you important? Yes, very important in such a case. Think about it for a moment. What would have happened if the commander and the soldiers had been allowed to speak "at eye level" without "distance" like friends? Can you train a friend to be a soldier?

Imagine for a second that you made an appointment with a friend and he or she was a minute late. What happens if you tell him or her, "You're a minute late! Now run for an hour!" I hope you're laughing really hard right now just imagining the situation.

You sure understand that you would not have any friends left if you treated them that way.

The point is: the way you behave (B) + the environment (E) + what you communicate (C) = the advantage of achieving the desired result (AR).

B+E+C=AR

B- behavior (your mindset and energy are important because in relation to social norms, behavior is a physical and emotional activity)
E- environment
C- communication
AR- advantage result

As an entrepreneur, business owner, or manager, you are a leader. I'm sure part of your business today is being run with virtual calls.

If there is a feeling that your staff is tired during the conversation, not showing interest, lacking concentration, not feeling comfortable, etc., there are a number of things you need to pay attention to. I will expand on this in the next chapter, which is entirely dedicated to Zoom and will provide everything you need to know in order to fulfill the equation of **B+E+C=AR.**

> **Action Step #1**
> Answer as detailed as possible.
> 1. How do I want others to see me?
> 2. What items can I add to my stage that will help me convey the feeling I want to give?
> 3. Close your eyes for a few minutes and imagine the ideal situation of how the other person sees you.

If you would like to get more information and learn more about these strategies, Shiran coaches people all over the world and has established a FREE Facebook group on non-verbal skills and techniques to help businesses and entrepreneurs develop their body language skills. *Shiran teaches Businesses & Online Entrepreneurs how to articulate with non-verbal communication, by developing confidence skills, decoding human behavior & Body Language Perspective, allowing them to understand & deliver the UNSPOKEN message while increasing their impact & profit.*

Click here to join her FREE group: [UNSPOKEN Decoding Human Behavior & Body Language for Business Success](#). Or email Shiran at Shiranunspoken@gmail.com for more details.

Make sure to answer all questions in order to join the group, and please mention the word "UNSPOKEN" so I'll know you've read this book.

Chapter 2.
Zoom In

I attend Zoom calls often. The ability to "read the room" is different. We are not present in the same environment, the participants' microphones are muted, we can't hear their child screaming in the background or them legging when you tell a joke. We are in front of a camera, and most of the time we are seen from the chest area and up.

Think about your last Zoom call and ask yourself:
What created interest for you?
What made you focus immediately?
What gave you feelings that you interpreted as positive?

You can add these answers to your answers from action step #1 from the previous chapter. As you progress through the book, you will be able to create the image you want to show.

You can design your Zoom appointments, but beyond preparing the environment, your non-verbal communication will be essential for conveying your message.

2.1 - Start with a smile

A smile is one of the most powerful triggers. We learn to mirror a smile in the early stages of infancy.
Close your eyes for 10 seconds and think of a cute smiling baby.

Did you smile? Most likely yes. We are evolutionarily wired to respond to a smile.

Furthermore, the smile directly affects our mood because it releases hormones like endorphins, oxytocin, serotonin, dopamine, and more which give a high feeling and can even ease pain.

If you meet a friend and he walks towards you and smiles, do you usually smile back? If you are not angry with him, there is a very high probability that you will smile back because your subconscious mind understands "he or she is happy to see me." We are human and we want and need to be loved and to feel connected, like we belong and are important. We want other people to see us and understand us.

You must concentrate for a moment on the next questions. Do you work better when you are happy or sad? Calm or nervous? In a good mood or in a bad mood?

We are all more motivated when we are in a good mood, calm, and happy. Why is it important? You are a leader! How do you want your people to feel?

You have the power to make others smile, feel better, and work better.
Think for a moment about the next time you are in a Zoom with your team. You smile and say hello to everyone and then do the following exercise with them:

Set a timer for 5 minutes and tell everyone not to stop smiling for the next 5 minutes. In addition, they should imagine the team members making funny faces. Tell them to unmute themselves and listen to the giggles.

What a funny way to start such a meeting? you may wonder.

You can add some humor of your own... "Even though the Zoom session is recorded, I do not collect dental information about you. You all work hard, and in challenging times I appreciate each and every one of you and you all deserve a break to laugh and smile."

You made them smile (release hormones that give a good feeling). You also told them, "I see you, appreciate you, and you are important." Do you think after these 5 minutes they will like you a little more? Will they be more attentive to the conversation? Will they be motivated to do a good job? And the price you paid to get it all was just 5 minutes of smiling.

Remember that if you smile more each day, you will be happier.

2.2 - Moving forward

Were you ever in a Zoom call and one of the participants started moving while holding the phone with the camera? Did it immediately grab your attention?

Of course, but do you know why?

Our brain is designed to protect us and help us survive. When there is movement of a person, animal, or any object, the brain immediately focuses on the movement to make sure we are safe.

Similarly, if there is fire in our field of vision, we are drawn to observe the fire. The flame creates movement, and we know that fire is dangerous. But equally we also know that fire distributes light and heat and helps man survive for years. When we think "light," we think "good." When we think "warmth," we also think "pleasant."

What if you want to convey warmth, comfort, and goodness? What if in your background there was a fireplace, or even candles?

Would it give the desired feeling and in addition create a little more focus to your square on the screen?

It probably would.

The movement creates interest and attracts focus.
Since in most Zoom conversations participants are sitting (static), and usually the person hosting the call is also sitting, we see from the chest up, and the sitting position creates a natural desire to place our hands on the chair handles or on our abdomen or leg area, which creates a situation where the hands are out of the frame.

If you want to create more focus, it's literally in your hands!

2.3 - Hand gestures

Our hands can perform movement without much effort, so naturally we tend to use our hands when we talk.

When the brain perceives the appearance of palms, you are telling the other person: "I have nothing to hide." It creates a sense of calm. When a cop says "hands up!" do you raise your hands with clenched fists or an open hand? Is the palm or the back of the palm facing the policeman?
The hands are open and the palm faces the policeman's field of vision because you are saying, "I have nothing to hide. I do not pose a threat."

In many cases, when there is unreliability, the person will hide his hands. Remember that in a Zoom call, the view is limited, so make sure to use your hands in the frame, especially when you are talking. This will help you attract focus, create more interest, and provide a sense of credibility.

The next thing you should know is how to use your hands to convey the right message. When we speak in front of an audience, we feel exposed. As you already know at this point in the book, our body language reveals what we feel.

So how does our body usually react when we feel exposed or threatened? Our natural tendency is to "reduce" ourselves; we shrink and converge. It is an evolutionary, natural defense mechanism designed to protect us.

In certain situations in life, especially in front of other people, we do not want to show weakness, fear, or embarrassment, etc.

Using your hands will help you channel your feelings into hand movement and create an open body language that conveys self-confidence.

Don't forget that we are all human and at certain moments, the ability to be vulnerable will indicate strength rather than weakness. A simple example of this could be a person standing in front of people and saying, "sorry, I was wrong" or "I failed" or sharing a personal story that carries a lot of pain within it.

We are human and connect through emotions. We have all felt failure, pain, fear, sadness, loss, anger, and also success, pleasure, courage, joy, love, hope, motivation, peace, etc.

Indeed, no human being experiences life exactly as another human being experiences it, and everyone has their own story. But, if I exclude any abnormal disorder, it can be said that we have all felt the same feelings at one time or another. Maybe in different situations and maybe at different points in our lives, but we know how the emotion feels.

Our hands say a lot! They can convey feelings and emotions nonverbally.
How would you feel if two people were standing on the side talking (you can't hear them) and one of them pointed at you?

Would you feel uncomfortable? As if you were being accused and you need to defend yourself? Embarrassed?

All these feelings because of one finger? Now you can imagine what the power of the hand is.

Great! So now it's time to learn how to use this superpower.

Most of the time, we will want to keep our hands open.
When someone gives you something, do you take it with an open hand or with a clenched hand? And when you give? The opening hand releases the object so that the other can receive.

Horizontal hand gestures - Giving and receiving are usually gentle movements made on the horizontal plane. Therefore, when we give information, explain, or invite, we usually use horizontal hand gestures.
Horizontal hand gestures are mediation gestures that help you convey a message between you and the other.

Vertical hand gestures - If the horizontal movements are bridging, then what is the meaning of vertical movements?

The vertical movements emphasize movements.
Think for a moment about an angry man who slams his hand on a table. What does the gesture symbolize? A hand pounding hard on the table? It is a vertical movement (designed to emphasize) that transmits the intensity of anger.

But timing is also essential. Have you ever been in a situation where someone was angry and pounded his hand on the table? At the time the words were said? Before the time the words were said? Or after the words were said?

Timing has great meaning! Most often, if the pounding action was done before, it may indicate advance planning and insincerity or a desire to attract attention.

If the act of pounding was done in time, it usually reveals the emotion and the verbal message matches the non-verbal message. Therefore, it indicates a real feeling, and the person is indeed angry.

If the pounding action was done after, it will usually indicate that anger is an exaggeration designed to disguise something else, and now you just have to figure out what.

The vertical hand gestures are meant to pinpoint the words and emphasize them.

Think about holding a small marble at the tip of your fingers. This movement creates a point, even if not all the fingers participate in holding the small marble and even if only the thumb and forefinger hold the marble and the rest of the fingers open (creates the OK sign).
With this point, you can pinpoint and emphasize the important words in the message you want to convey and in addition attract attention and focus.
Think of the dot on your fingertips as a laser dot. What happens to us when there is a point that catches our attention and also creates movement? Our eye focuses on the dot and we pay attention.

We can also create a lot of interest when we hold the palm slightly rounded, as if we are holding an imaginary ball in our hand. Try to talk about a particular idea and hold your hand in such a way as if you are holding your idea in the palm of your hand. It will draw attention to your idea and message.

The use of hands is necessary for our non-verbal communication, but there are a number of things that are important not to do with the hands.

1. Hiding the hands in pockets, behind the back, or behind a table or object can sometimes indicate insincerity.

2. Unwanted touches. In many stressful situations, people will "play" with the fingers, rub hand in hand, touch the face and hair on the neck, arrange clothes and touch jewelry such as a watch, necklace, or ring. All of these will usually indicate discomfort. And when we do not feel comfortable, the one who looks at us feels it, and that will usually make the other person feel uncomfortable as well.

3. Inadequacy. When the mouth says one thing and the hand or the non-verbals

signify something else. For example, if you say, "My business is growing fast" and your hand makes downward movement (crashing) instead of upward (taking off), it shows unreliability that strongly indicates a lie. In the case of inadequacy, we may treat the non-verbal communication as truth.

2.4 – Posture

Our posture reflects whether we are confident, threatening, reluctant, uncomfortable, scared or just tired.

Naturally, we want to show confidence in ourselves. If we look at the postures of famous leaders, politicians, actors, and singers, we can see that most of them have a presence that conveys self-confidence.

So what does self-confidence look like in body language? (This explanation is true for both sitting and standing.)

Upright back, shoulders open, chin parallel to the floor, no "barrier" between me and the other, free hands without crossing hands... This is a myth! People believe that crossing your hands indicates a lie, but in fact it is like a self-hug that we use when we feel vulnerable. We do it even when we are cold, for example.

Try not to hide the abdomen and chest area. Also, do not hide by standing or sitting behind objects. In Zoom calls, the field of view is usually from chest height and up. If the hands are combined or placed on the abdomen, the shoulders can appear converged and slightly inward.

A simple way to remind yourself to sit this way is to simply decide that your chair is the throne and you should act accordingly. Be the king! Be the queen!

Whenever you want to change your body language, you can simply create an image in your head that will both make the experience more fun and make it easier for you to remember. Tell yourself a story and become the main character.

Note the position of the camera. You want to place the camera at eye level or slightly higher (which will remind you to sit upright). Usually, the body will turn to the camera, but sometimes—especially in one-on-one conversations—if you feel the other person feels uncomfortable, you can turn the body about 10 to 15 degrees to offer a more comfortable and casual feeling.

2.5 - Tone of voice

First of all, you need to make sure that you are using a proper microphone and that you are heard well.

Tone of voice is driven out of our subconscious, and therefore it will reveal emotion if we pay attention to volume, rhythm, tremble and the fragility in the voice.

Do not surprise others with your voice when a microphone is located close to you. In a personal conversation, the person has distance from you, and you do not speak directly into their ear. In Zoom calls, many of the participants use headphones. Even if they are not, they are sitting next to the computer (close to the speakers), so try not to shout but also not to whisper. Be clear and do not rush too much. With this technology, there can be delays sometimes.

Your breathing is a major component of your tone of voice. When people are stressed, anxious, or excited, we breathe faster and superficially. It is felt immediately, and sometimes we do not have enough air to finish a sentence (sometimes this may even indicate a lie). Be aware of your breathing.

One of the most effective exercises to practice speaking with slow breathing is simply to sing.

This helps strengthen the diaphragm, which helps to expel air during the breathing process.

It is recommended that we use the tone of speech to emphasize important words by increasing the tone when the word is spoken louder or by pausing (which will create a bit of tension).
For example, imagine I tell you that a few days ago, I got a phone call and on the other side of the line was a friend I had not heard from for years. He sounded a bit stressed and told me he really needed my help and then (louder)…(a few seconds of a pause).

Aren't you curious to know what happened next in the conversation?

We can create more interest in a conversation when we use our tone of voice to emphasize, or talk faster to be funny, or create a sense of a rush. We can also use our voices to calm others, like in meditation, slow speaking, and soft gentle tones.

2.6 - Facial Expressions

Dr. Paul Ekman is an expert on facial expressions. The TV series *Lie to Me,* which deals with solving crimes by using facial expression analysis is based on information that he discovered while researching facial expressions.

He also studied the face anatomy and how humans have 43 muscles in the face, and he found that there are more than ten thousand facial expressions, although not all of them indicate emotion.

But there are a number of facial expressions that are universal and which reveal an emotion that is significant for understanding human behavior.

In an article written by Dr. Paul Ekman, it is noted that the facial expressions that express anger, disgust, fear, pleasure, sadness, satisfaction, contempt, and surprise are universal.

In a Zoom call, we usually see facial expressions, but all the participants are muted so we do not hear a sound.
Will it help you to at least get to know these facial expressions?

Definitely! The ability to understand facial expressions will allow you to read the room better, ask better questions, or clarify what you have already said.

If you desire to transform your Zoom calls and would like to learn more about facial expressions, ask about my masterclass, Zoom In to the UNSPOKEN Business Success. Email Shiran at Shiranunspoken@gmail.com for access.

Chapter 3.
7 Steps to Hire Smarter

Fraud—a 5-letter word that triggers fear in most people. The consequences of fraud can cause a great deal of damage. So when we bring someone into our lives, our homes, or our businesses, it is important that we keep ourselves as safe as possible.

It is much simpler to lie in writing, where the non-verbal communication is taken out of the picture and only the words, the 7% of our communication, remain. In fact, most people lie in their resumes about their experience (example: declare 5 years of seniority and actually have only 4) or character traits, empowering themselves to gain a relative advantage.

This chapter will give you the knowledge and tools so you can minimize this phenomenon in your own business.

Filtering recruitment is a struggle that exists for every business owner.

I want you to imagine the following scene:

Three months ago, you hired a new manager to your marketing team. On paper, their resume is perfect for what you need and they are exactly the person that you've been looking for. Maybe that person excelled in the job interview and was accepted for the position.

But now after three months you realize they don't have skills that you expected them to have. Maybe their values or personality aren't aligned with the company, and you have already invested so much money into their training, not to mention massive amounts of time! The time of your existing employees, the HR department, the managers who made the interview, the person who trained the new employee—that means many hours from their paychecks are now gone.

That really hurts, doesn't it?

Most businesses, when they hire someone, go through the same process:
1. Make a decision that you need to hire
2. Decide the skills that you want your new employee to have
3. Advertise an ad
4. Filter resumes
5. Conduct job interviews
6. Make the decision of who to hire among the people you interviewed.

Yet, we all know it doesn't end there. Once your new employee has been hired, there are still many expenses related to training, acquaintance with the company, and adaptation to the new work environment.

Here is an important question for you:

How much does it cost you if you hire the wrong person for a job?

If you consider all the expenses, from the moment you decided you needed to hire until the moment you realized after three months that the employee you hired did not meet the desired result, you have already spent tens of thousands of dollars, maybe even hundreds of thousands of dollars (depending on salaries and time of all concerned).

Would you like to know how to minimize that problem in your business and save a lot of money?

Let me tell you a secret—it all starts with one question:

- **At what stage in the process do you perform your employee's initial filtering?**

When I ask people that question, often the answer is, when they receive their resume. This is the most crucial mistake anyone who hires an employee can make.

As a matter of fact, you should filter your employees from the first second you made the decision that you need to hire.

That's why in this chapter, I will show you **7 Steps To Hire Smarter** that you can easily follow and apply in your business to act as an exceptional manager or business owner. This is exactly where you do not want to be like most managers, business owners, entrepreneurs, etc.

3.1 - STEP 1 - Wise Decision:

Making the decision that you need to hire requires you to ask yourself the following two questions:
   1. What position will that person have?
   2. What problems will this employee solve for me?
   3. How much money are you willing to pay for it?

3.2 - STEP 2 - The Employee Avatar:

Decide the **Skills**, **Values**, and **Personality** that you want your new employee to have.

Most managers, when they are deciding to hire, only take under consideration the skills that they want their new employee to have, and, as I said before, here we will learn how to be extraordinary so we can get extraordinary results.

SVP (**S**kills, **V**alues, **P**ersonality)

We spend many hours every week at work, so ideally, we want to hire people that we feel comfortable with during those hours; people we like to be around, because our environment and state of mind determine how well or how badly we perform during each day. That alone can significantly impact how much we love our jobs and whether we are happy to get up and go to work every morning.

That's why when you hire, it's very important to think about the values and the personality as well as the skills. Would you like to have the smartest and most qualified manager but with the personality that makes everybody else suffer? I bet you wouldn't want to have that person on your team.

It's very important to be very clear on the type of employee that you want to have; just like when you are setting a goal, you think about the desirable outcome. You should act the same when you are searching for employees.

The following action step will help you to narrow down your most desirable employee. You will use this list in the next step when you write your ad.

Action step #2

<u>Desirable Employee Hack</u>
Skills - Make a list of all the desirable skills that you want your employee to have. Now divide that list into 3 categories: "Must have," "Experience," and "Bonus."

Values - Make a list of all the desirable values that you want your employee to have. Now divide that list into 3 categories: "Must have," "Not acceptable," and "Bonus."

Personality - Think about the employees that you value the most or the people that you love the most and make a list of all their personality aspects that you absolutely love.

If you value and love them, that means that you like being around them, and you want to make sure that your ideal employee will be someone that you value.

Make a list of all the desirable personality qualities that you value the most in your employees and people that you love. Make another list of qualities that you don't like in other people and divide both lists into 3 categories: "Must have," "Not acceptable," and "Bonus."

Now you have a basic idea of the person that you want to hire, so keep that list.

3.3 - STEP 3 - Effective ad

Advertisement ads are very similar to the marketing process; even though many people think that the candidates should "promote" themselves in order to get the job, actually, in this phase, the advertiser is "selling" the position of the job and the company itself.

Keep in mind, however, that marketing the open position shouldn't be the main focus. If you want to see extraordinary results from your ad process, you must consider and try to target your **SVP** in your messaging.

Before you even start writing your ad, ask yourself: What are the desirable things that my ideal employee should have?

When you make your list, in order to choose the hook, you should include the following:
1. Income.
2. Benefits.
3. Work environment.

Add to your hook:
1. One "must have" (**S**kills)
2. One "must have" (**V**alues)
3. One "must have" (**P**ersonality)

Once you figure that out, write a title that will hook your ideal employee.
The right hook will immediately trigger desirable outcomes and emotions.

For example, if you're looking for a software engineer to lead a team, your hook could be: "If you are a loyal and high performing software engineer, we have a 6-figure offer for you to lead our team."

This is very different from saying:
"Required: A software engineer team manager for a Hi-Tech company"

In the first example, the main focus is on your target employee and what they desire. The second example focuses on what your company needs.

Here is the information that I'm getting from the first example:
- Loyal (**V**alues)
- High performer (**P**ersonality)
- Software engineer (**S**kills)
- 6 figures (Desirable outcome)
- Lead our team (what they will have to do in order to get the desirable outcome)

Warning: Different countries have different rules and laws, so make sure everything that you are writing doesn't break any local laws. I'm giving examples based on my knowledge, experience, and expertise. You are responsible for making sure that your ad doesn't break any local laws.

After you have written the desired title in the content of the message, you will describe the job and the requirements in order for them to receive the job, such as: degree, years of experience, how many work hours, etc.

In your message, add the **S V P** of your ideal employee from the list of "must" you created earlier.

This alone will attract your ideal employee, but at this point, there is another thing you need to do in order to filter the right person, avoid resume fraud, and protect the resources of your company.

I only share this secret with my clients, and if you are reading this book and you are serious and willing to apply the process, I would love to share the secret with you, too. Simply send me an email with the word "UNSPOKEN" and "I want to find out the ad secret."
shiranunspoken@gmail.com

3.4 - STEP 4 - Filtering resumes:

This is the stage where most businesses are just beginning to filter.

If you have done the previous steps, this step will be much easier and more efficient for you because the chance of meeting your ideal potential employee is significantly increased.

Let's think for a moment. What usually happens at this point?
Candidates send an email with a file of resumes attached.

The HR department reads and reviews the resumes and calls to coordinate a job interview with those suitable for the job.

- How many resumes were reviewed before finding a suitable person to see for a job interview?
- How long does it take for a meeting with one person to be scheduled in this process?
- Is there a way to pinpoint and shorten this process?

Definitely, here is the step that many businesses miss:

3.5 - STEP 5 - Automation and background check:

Yes, I hear you: "Automation for resume filtering? How do I do that?"

You will not believe how simple and effective it is.
Create a digital form with questions that will give you the desired indication of the **SVP** you are looking for.

Today, most ads are posted digitally on forums and websites. We see much fewer ads in print newspapers.
It is important to note that in order to find the ideal employee, you need to understand where that employee will be looking for work. Which forums will they check?
In which groups are they members on social networks, etc.? When you have this information, you can easily attach a link to fill out the form you created.

Many digital forms will give you a comparison of the candidates' answers. This will give you an indication of your top candidates without the HR department having to filter dozens of resumes to find the top candidates. Let technology save time for you.

How much time and resources for your company have you saved so far?

I'm sure a lot! But the process does not end here.

You still need to verify that the information provided to you and on which your knowledge of the candidate is based is correct.

This is the time to do a background check.

You can hire a company to do it for you or do it yourself.

If you decide to do it yourself, use all the information provided to you so far and cross-reference the information.

Try to find out:
- Is the information provided accurate?
- Did the candidate have a different name in the past? (Was the name changed? For example, as a result of marriage?) Sometimes, if an offense was committed, the person may have changed the name in order to obscure the past.
- Write down any questions you would like to clarify with the candidate. These questions will be asked during the job interview so you can observe the candidate's responses.

3.6 - STEP 6- Have a friendly conversation instead of just a job interview:

When people feel comfortable with you, they are more likely to cooperate and share more details willingly.

This does not mean that you will have to invite them to a restaurant to conduct the job interview. It simply means that you need to learn a few simple principles regarding your body language so that you create an open environment and the candidate will feel comfortable reflecting the same openness from the environment.

Consider that in most job interviews, on the other hand, the candidates feel that they will be examined which increases the level of tension. This sometimes results in the candidate sending a wrong or unintentional message. During the interview we want to "surprise" with questions that will reveal how the candidate responds or reacts in different situations and then to ask ourselves "Is that the manager or employee I want?".

The amount of information you can find out about a person in a friendly conversation is significantly more valuable than if you present yourself as an authoritative figure examining the candidates.

The authoritative approach will provide you with short and focused answers to your questions, but a friendly conversation will reveal more information as the candidate feels comfortable sharing more extended answers.

I learned this technique when I worked for 10 years preventing terrorism in aviation.

As part of my job, I had to decide within 7 minutes whether the person standing in front of me was a risk to the flight or to the passengers. I was sometimes required to create a friendly conversation with them or to look from the side and pay attention to the body language, environment, and potential risk, checking people and their belongings at the strictest level. In this field of work, there is no room for error. The result of negligence at work can cost human lives.

During my years on the job, I was involved in more flights than I can count. This means that hundreds of thousands of people arrived safely at their destinations and back to their families because of the rigor with which my team and I performed our work.

Because the security process used by the Israeli defense system is classified, I cannot share information from friendly conversations I conducted directly.

That is why in my workshops, I help your company create the right techniques that will reveal the information you need based on my years of experience.

Some of the information that was revealed through this technique include:
- Hidden relationships between people
- Relationships to hostile elements
- Information on the location of weapons
- Attempts to gather intelligence information for the purpose of carrying out an attack
- Fake documents
- And sometimes even information such as infidelity between spouses, theft, use of prohibited substances, and so much more.

In order to have a friendly conversation, you need to understand where you are starting. The intention is not only to say hello but to gauge how much the person in front of you feels comfortable with you.

Imagine that you have invited a candidate for a job interview.
The candidate comes from an understanding that you will examine him and his suitability for the position.

For the most part, the candidate feels "smaller" in such a position, while the interviewer feels in a position of power.

Often when we are faced with a stressful situation, our body language will transmit discomfort, and when the person in front of you feels uncomfortable, you will see that he will "reduce" himself. The posture will not be upright, and the shoulders will roll inwards, the chin will be closer to the chest, and often the hands will be hidden or creating a barrier between you two.

Let me be completely honest with you. You can learn and memorize what each movement means and examine the person in front of you using this knowledge. But the truth is that you will probably get it wrong, not because you are not a body language expert but because you will focus only on what you are looking for, as that's what you will find.

The most important thing you can learn is to pay attention to the overall picture—body language changes depending on emotions, environment, culture, status, the person's health, etc.

We all utilize non-verbal communication on a daily basis, and our subconscious mind knows exactly how to recognize the non-verbal.

Have you ever been told something from someone, and, even though you could not prove otherwise, you just knew he was not being honest? How did you know?

Did you ever call a friend and, just by hearing their "hello," you knew something was wrong? How did you know?

You see, you already know non-verbal communication, now you just need to pay attention to details and trust your gut. But of course you also need to learn what to pay attention to and how to find the real perspective, not just yours.

When I meet any person, I'm trying to have a clear perspective. That's why I treat the encounter like I know nothing about non-verbal communication. I study the reactions, I notice the rhythm of breathing, the rhythm of speech, posture, hand movements, body touches (pats of hands on thigh, touch of hand in hand, touches in face, ears in neck, etc.). I establish for myself a guideline that is specifically tailored to the person in front of me.

This is critical because, while most sources tell you that when a person touches the neck, it shows embarrassment or discomfort, you will sometimes meet a person who touches the neck in response to physiological pain and not because there is embarrassment. Many people may misinterpret the situation if they believe that touching the neck only means embarrassment or discomfort.

Body language varies from person to person. Also, women have a more "reserved" body language than men. It is not possible to include all the rules on all human beings; we are similar, but each of us is also different.

Everyone is unique; our appearance is not the same, our voice is not the same, so why do we expect that our body language will be identical with unambiguous meaning?

Do you expect an introverted person to use the same hand gestures, posture, or tone of voice as a politician, for example?
No.
Why not? Because they are different—we are all different.

I know at the moment you're probably thinking to yourself, "This is harder than I thought" or "How am I supposed to know if there are no conclusive movements?"

In fact, it is simple. Here are the steps you need to take:

1. Trust your gut feeling.
2. Treat only the facts and not the assumptions that you come up with ahead of time.
3. Listen and observe.
4. Create a guideline.
5. Ask open-ended questions.

Remember, you do not have to be an expert, you just need to be aware, pay attention, and look for fit and mismatch between the verbal and non-verbal. Of course, as you educate yourself more, you will observe and practice, and the non-verbal will become an integral part of understanding communication and a smart advantage.

3.7 - STEP 7 - Making the decision of who to hire

If you have followed all the steps so far, the decision at this stage will be much simpler for you.
At this point, you need to decide based on the data you have received so far who is the leading candidate for you. Make sure to stick to the **SVP** and trust your gut feeling.

If you would like to transform your team hiring process and learn more about the UNSPOKEN in your business, ask me about my masterclass, HIRE SMARTER - The

UNSPOKEN Business Success, email Shiranunspoken@gmail.com.

Chapter 4.
Fearless Impact

Do you know what the main emotion is that prevents us from taking action?

Fear. That's right, or anxiety, to be more accurate, because there's a big difference between those two. In both cases, similar symptoms appear. With fear, there is an immediate danger or risk to your well-being, and anxiety draws fear that is driven by our thoughts and emotions and the way we process them in our minds.

One of the best examples is fear of speaking in front of an audience, people, or a camera. That is actually anxiety, and it's more common than you think.

Have you ever stood on a stage in front of an audience, posted a video, or went live on social media?

If your answer is "no" ask yourself: "Why not?" I bet you will find that there is fear and anxiety behind that decision.

If your answer is "yes," ask yourself: "How did it feel the first time? How much courage did it take for me to press that button or step on that stage? Why did I do that anyway?

In this case, you probably summoned stronger emotions for something that you wanted, desired, or needed, and you knew how to find the courage and not give up.

Let's take social media as an example: Were you afraid of one of the following?

- The camera will break down during the broadcast
- Low battery on your phone
- The possibility that you would lose broadcast connection

Sounds a little bit irrational, right? Well actually, I had a Zoom call with a client, and during that one 20-minute call I had three power blackouts. Our call was disconnected three times, and that's how a 20-minute call turned into a 40-minute call. As a business owner I've learned something from that experience and I purchased two backup batteries one for my computer and one for my wifi device to minimize the inconvenience.

And yet, all those reasons aren't the main reason that we are afraid when it comes to talking live in front of an audience, whether in person or on camera.

So what makes it so hard for so many people to stand in front of an audience and be exposed to the public eye?

Are you concerned about what people might think of you?

That people will make fun of you or judge you?

Are you concerned that you will forget what you wanted to say and that you will fail?

Are you afraid that there's a lot more to learn about the subject, and that you just aren't qualified yet to teach?

I asked many people about why they are afraid of standing in front of an audience.

Most people are afraid of how other people will look at them or what other people think about them, but they are also concerned about how they look on camera; "I look tired," "I'm overweight," "I have ugly eyebrows," etc. Those are some of the reasons that people told me about, and they hold them back from showing up on camera for their businesses.

We are not afraid of the action, we are afraid of the emotion that might appear as a result of that action. Once we understand the emotion, we can reframe it and reverse the way that we feel and empower ourselves instead making ourselves more anxious.

We can reframe by using our mindset, which basically means reframing our thoughts to gain a different perspective. For example, if you are afraid that people might laugh at you, here is what you need to do. You need to separate the facts from the emotions:

- Fact: You don't know what the future holds.
- Fact: You don't know what other people think, you can't read their minds.
- What if people love you?
- What if they adore you?

Now think carefully about this question: Are you afraid of the failure or of the success?

Here is the link to download my "Unstoppable Courage," a short read that will help you find the right mindset to find the courage that you need.

Unstoppable Courage

So all that you need to do is reframe your questions into better questions that will give you better answers. This will drive you to be courageous and not to give up in the face of fear and anxiety.

In addition, if you use your body language, you can change your feelings even faster, because movement creates energy. It releases hormones in our bodies and we can change how we feel just by acting in certain ways. For example, if you sit in front of a mirror and smile for 5 minutes, you will feel much happier after you are done. Just by watching yourself smile, and just by smiling, you are releasing certain hormones into your body. Like I mentioned in chapter 2, this creates what you feel when you are happy.

You can also watch the TED talk "Your body language may shape who you are" by Amy Cuddy on YouTube. She shared how to use power posters to change our feelings.

We can cultivate the right tools to cope. This doesn't mean that you won't feel fear or anxiety, but it does mean that you will be able to act in spite of the fear.

The way we use our communication, verbal and non-verbal, also can determine how the viewer feels.

If now I stand in front of an audience and I look for a volunteer, what will happen?

If I say, "Who wants to be my first victim today?" while I half smile and rub my hands, do you think I will get any volunteers? Probably not. Well, I tried it several times in my workshops and no one volunteered. When I did get someone brave enough, they came with a lot of hesitation.

On the other hand, if I said, "Who wants to be the first courageous person to come up here and change their body language?" with a smile and open body language, I will get a completely different result. People won't feel so uncomfortable volunteering because people would rather be courageous than a victim.

So what did I actually do?

Just through the way that I phrased my question and used non-verbal communication, I triggered and affected the way people feel about taking a certain action.

By using the word "victim" and matching my body language to something that seems sleazy, I triggered fear. That wasn't inviting people to take the action.

In addition to using my words and body language, I can use my tone of voice when I'm saying "victim" and I can make it sound scary. But when I'm saying "courageous," I can make it sound exciting, and that won't feel like a threat to you.

By using the word "courageous" and keeping open and welcoming body language, I framed the fear and triggered courage that allowed people to take action.

What we say and how we act when we say it will affect immediately the other person's emotions, and, as a result, their actions.

Now think about what you can control (at a certain level), how you make other people feel and respond to you.

Do you realize that understanding human behavior is extremely important for a business owner to become a successful entrepreneur?

You're already using body language as a daily skill, but whether you do that right or not is the same as whether you choose to use your words in an articulate way or not.

If you're reading this book, you understand the language in which it is written. Let's take English as an example.

If you walk down the street and a couple passes you by speaking English, even if you aren't trying to listen to their conversation, you are still able to understand their words.

It works exactly the same with body language. Even though you are not focusing on trying to read other people's body language, you still pick a lot of information up on other people just from their body language and tone of voice. It's the same for them regarding you; people are picking up a lot of information from your body language without you or them even realizing that they are doing so. It's a subconscious process that automatically happens in our brains.

If you focus each time on being a leader, and also think about how you want your people to feel and not just what information you want to convey to them, it will be easier for you to show up with confidence and a smile. You will create the desired emotion and context that will give you a smart advantage to lead them to better results.

If you are struggling with showing up on camera for your business and would like to learn more about it, *Shiran teaches Businesses & Online Entrepreneurs how to articulate with non-verbal communication, by developing confidence skills, decoding human behavior & Body Language Perspective, allowing them to understand & deliver the UNSPOKEN message while increasing their impact & profit..*

Click here to join her FREE group: <u>UNSPOKEN Decoding Human Behavior & Body Language for Business Success</u>. Or email Shiranunspoken@gmail.com for more details.

Chapter 5.
The Unspoken Leader Skills

What does a positive impression mean to you?

Does it mean appearing with confidence?

How do other people respond to what you say?

Do people see you as an authority figure?

Actually, one of the most important things to understand is that the first few seconds in a first meeting determine a person's first impression of you.

Mark Bowden is an author and body language and human behavior expert. He wrote in his book that 100% of a first impression is immediately determined by our primitive minds based on non-verbal communication.

We often subconsciously examine the people we meet. How they walk, what they wear, their appearance, movements, eye gaze, sound of their voice, etc.

It is often easier for us to like someone who is "similar" to us, whether in the style of dress, behavior, etc., because we recognize these aspects as something familiar.

Have you ever judged someone just by what they were wearing?

We've all done it before. We're used to seeing a certain look and then something else comes along that we categorize as very unusual and a thought goes through our heads: "What the hell is she wearing?" We reject a person even before we interact with him directly.

I served two years in the Israeli military and 10 more years in defense work preventing terrorism in aviation worldwide.

Body language is a skill I practiced for many years, and it guided me every day while I did my job, and every day since.

Understanding non-verbal communication is not just knowing if someone is lying or trying to deceive you. Once we understand how to use our body language to deliver a message that we want to convey, we also learn how to influence someone's emotions, and, as a result, influence their actions or decisions.

Now I know that you might be thinking right now, "it sounds like a fraud, I don't want to make someone do something just because I want to get the result I want. It's selfish." But it's not so complicated. For example, how do we treat people when we are happy? How do other people react to the way we treat them?

If you think about it, you will realize that we transmit our feelings and energies to other people and they react to us based on what we show them from their own perspective. So what happens if we stand in front of the camera and we feel insecure or uncomfortable? Well, it would actually make the viewer feel uncomfortable because it would be like watching someone suffering. Hopefully, you don't want to see someone else suffer.

Just by understanding basic body language and how to use your tone of voice, you can make a huge difference with how you connect with other people and how they engage with you.

The very first few seconds when you meet a person, the way that you greet them, the way that you show up in front of them; all of these things determine most of the positive impressions you can make.

The mindset, or way we think and process information, can change psychology, and how we use our body language, as I explained earlier, can also change how we feel. It works both ways. Being aware of your body language will benefit you, and with attention and practice, you will begin to notice much more about the body language of other people, too.

We can use our body language to make a positive impression on someone, including our posture, facial expressions, hand gestures, and, of course, the tone of our voice.

5.1 - How to deal with unwanted situations – insecurity, mistakes, and right body language

In some situations, you might feel insecure, ashamed, uncomfortable, or even embarrassed. Our instinct is to "reduce" ourselves, but in those cases, we don't want people to see those things because it's not about our vulnerability. It's about how we feel in a certain situation that might cause us to use uninviting body language.

Let's take, for example, a situation where you are making a one-on-one Zoom call to pitch an offer to a potential client.

Did you ever ask yourself, "What do I look like when I'm asking for money?"

Remember that we are asking for money in exchange for services or products.

We all have different limiting beliefs deep in our subconscious minds, and those beliefs often stem from our childhoods. It's not that simple to break those limitations. You might have heard that "money doesn't grow on trees." Maybe you've heard that "you need to work really hard to make money," or that "rich people are born rich, or they must be hustling somehow or cheating or just not being honest."

I've seen many cases where people are asking for money in such an uncertain way that the other person can immediately sense that it's not about the number, or about the price; it's about how they feel asking that price for their services and products.

When we are asking for money, we are exposing our self-image and our self confidence. We are basically telling the other person why we are worth that price. That might be an indicator to the other person that we are not sure, or that we are insecure about our capabilities, and if we are doubting our capabilities, why should they trust us?

In some cases, the other person might feel that we are trying to trick them or lie to them.

Asking for money is one of the main things that you need to feel comfortable with as an entrepreneur or a business owner. If you have a problem with this, you will find it very difficult to get paying clients.

Here, you need to use your body language so you can close the deal and make more money.

When you're just about to offer your product or service, you actually want to create a different FOCUS point. It's not about the money. You must know what problem you are solving for them, and what it's worth to them.

People usually will keep their focus on the few last words that you are saying, so if you end by saying, my price is $4,000, followed by silence, naturally, the other person is focusing on the number. Now, all they can think about is the price, and most likely they will ask a follow-up question regarding the price. In this case, you might find yourself in an uncomfortable situation trying to justify or to defend yourself for asking that price.

You need to change the focus to emphasize the value the individual is getting from working with you or buying your products, so don't make the price one of the last words you say. Say something before the price, then say the price, and then continue to say another thing after the price.

This is the service (or product) that I'm offering...the price is...and that includes.

So, if you arrange your sentence that way, you won't get stuck right after you say the price, and instead of focusing on the price, your customer will follow you because you still have a lot to say about the value of your service. The customers' questions are now more likely to be about the value or importance of them buying your product.

Regarding body language, there are a few things you want to avoid when you state the price:

- Don't touch your face.
- Don't start itching.
- Don't move in an uncomfortable way.
- Don't shrug your shoulders.
- Don't clear your throat.

This type of behavior often indicates stress, so try to maintain the same body language and tone of voice that you've used so far. If you change your body language after you start talking about the price, that is a strong indicator for the other person who is watching you to think that you are feeling uncomfortable or insecure. That will give them the wrong impression, and this is definitely not the message that you want to convey.

Make sure to continue with the same body language that you've had all along.

In some cases, we might speak and barely move, then just when we are about to say the price, our body language shifts to being aggressive; that shows that we are making an effort to sell.

At times, our tone of voice will indicate how we feel about a price. For example, we come to the price point in a sales pitch and suddenly start to speak more quietly. That indicates to the other person that you are insecure about the words you are saying. Perhaps you feel the price is too high? Maybe you are insecure about your capabilities? So why would your client trust you?

It's very simple to avoid this reaction; all you need to do is contact a magician and tell him what you want to change. Hahaha. I'm just checking you're still with me. Like anything else in life, it's necessary to practice. Did I make you laugh again? You like me a little more now! (Thank you!) You can practice in front of a mirror, in front of a friend, in front of the camera, etc. It might be uncomfortable at first, but after a while, it will become natural to you because you will shift your focus away from the number to the actual value and what your clients get out of doing business with you. The big message should be the benefits they are about to receive.

Don't ever place the money as the most important thing when you sell. Don't say things like, "You definitely should join us, it's really cheap compared to other people or this other program." You need to understand that if that person wants to work with you, it's not because your price is cheaper. Most people won't purchase from you just because your price is cheaper, and neither do I. I want to know what you are giving me and whether I need or want it.

5.2 - Better connection – 5 tips to make people relate to you

- Be sure to listen; people like to feel that you see, listen, and understand them.
- Ask open questions about things they say to show interest and to discover more information.
- Mirror: Say the three last words or the three most significant words in a

different tone as you are asking a question.
- Keep open body language and try to avoid creating a barrier.
- Talk to their emotional brain and behavior.

Action step #3

Now that you have the necessary information, just like in Action step #1, write down in full detail:

- How do you want others to see you?

- How will your environment, your frame, express this?

- Sit for a few minutes, close your eyes, and imagine yourself when you have already achieved the desired result. This practice is essential, because the mind does not know how to distinguish between reality and imagination. Being able to see yourself achieving the result will help you get there faster.

If you are the decision-maker in your business and you would like to have a FREE 20-minute consult call, email
Shiranunspoken@gmail.com

Acknowledgements

Thank you! To my whole family for the support and help and love.
Thank you to my dog Poonch who always makes me happy who loves unconditionally and is an integral part of the family.

Special thanks to my brother Avichai (Avi) Cohen - I won a brother with a huge heart, who makes sure I always know that no matter what happens I can always turn to him and I will be welcomed with open arms.

Avichai, thank you that ever since I remember myself you have always done your best to help and make sure I am safe. Thank you for always being my safety net. I love you my brother!

A huge thanks to my mentors Tony Robbins, Dean Graziosi, and Russell Brunson, who together created the KBB (Knowledge Broker Blueprint), and to everyone involved in the KBB community mission to make self-education the new norm. Through this community, I've learned how to scale my business and have met incredible people that I'm so grateful to have in my life!

An enormous THANK YOU to my mentor and soul sister, Melanie Warner, founder of the Defining Moments book series. Writing a book with your program has become a simple and focused task. The love, appreciation, and respect I have for you is far beyond what I can describe in a few sentences.

I love you, sister! And I am grateful that you are part of my journey.

Thank you so much to Emily Crawford-Margison for editing this book. Since I'm not a native English speaker, your suggestions helped me to convey my thoughts in a way that is understandable cross-culturally and resonates with readers.

My dear friend and mentor Sandra Haseley, the founder of "Sandra Haseley + co.", I'm so grateful to have you in my life! Thank you! Your support, love, and guidance is a bright light in my path at every stage. You are the business strategist and branding GODDESS! I'm honored to learn from you and so lucky to call you my friend. I love you forever, sister! Thank you for letting me into your beautiful heart and walking alongside me during this life journey.

Thank you to the amazing "Generation Impact" founding team of three: Shane Therault, David Waldy, and the one-and-only Sandra Haseley. Working with you has been an eye-opening experience that allowed me to gain different perspectives and strategies while growing my business. I am so grateful that our paths have crossed, and I am privileged to be part of your client family.

Thank you, QUEEN! My mentor and friend Lisa Hyde, the founder of "THE CONFIDENCE CROWN." Your huge heart, endless caring, and precious wisdom are so valuable to me. I appreciate and deeply love you! Having you in my life makes a huge difference, and I'm grateful for every moment.

A huge THANK YOU! to the three foundingWonder Women: Lisa Hyde, Jessica Mejia- Fahnestock, and Lynee Palacios. Thank you for your support, honesty, transparency, and for the safe place you created! Your program and guidance provided massive value for my business and personal growth.

About the Author

Sometimes life presents you with excruciating challenges, but years later, in retrospect, you can appreciate the resilience that brought you through.

Shiran is the living example of this. She was born and raised in Israel, where violence was present in her life, at home, and outside of the household.

Growing up in a country where terrorism and war are no strangers, she lost two cousins in two different terrorist attacks. From a young age, she learned to observe and look for the "attacker."

Shiran served two years in the Israeli military and 10+ years in defense work preventing terrorisem in aviation worldwide. She received a Certificate of Excellence for this role.

Shiran has visited many countries and has vigorously studied human behavior, body language, self-defense, and many other tools.

Following a car accident in March 2013, she had to relinquish this role in order to focus on recovering from the injuries caused by the accident.

Shiran coaches people all over the world and teaches Businesses & Online Entrepreneurs how to articulate with non-verbal communication, by developing confidence skills, decoding human behavior & Body Language Perspective, allowing them to understand & deliver the UNSPOKEN message while increasing their impact & profit.

Shiran is a #1 international bestselling author of the book, *Become Brilliant: Roadmap From Fear to Courage*.

Shiran is also a workshop trainer for Tony Robbins and Dean Graziosi on their KBB (Knowledge Broker Blueprint).

About Defining Moments Press

Built for aspiring authors who are looking to share transformative ideas with others throughout the world, Defining Moments Press offers life coaches, healers, business professionals, and other non-fiction or self-help authors a comprehensive solution to get their book published without breaking the bank or taking years.

Defining Moments Press prides itself on bringing readers and authors together to find tools and solutions for everyday problems.

As an alternative to self-publishing or signing with a major publishing house, we offer full profits to our authors, low-priced author copies, and simple contract terms.

Most authors get stuck trying to navigate the technical end of publishing. The comprehensive publishing services offered by Defining Moments Press mean that your book will be designed by an experienced graphic artist, available in printed, hard copy format, and coded for all eBook readers, including the Kindle, iPad, Nook, and more.

We handle all of the technical aspects of your book creation so you can spend more time focusing on your business that makes a difference for other people.

Defining Moments Press founder, publisher, and #1 bestselling author Melanie Warner has over 20 years of experience as a writer, publisher, master life coach, and accomplished entrepreneur.

You can learn more about Warner's innovative approach to self-publishing or take advantage of free trainings and education at: MyDefiningMoments.com.

Defining Moments Book Publishing

If you're like many authors, you have wanted to write a book for a long time, maybe you have even started a book...but somehow, as hard as you have tried to make your book a priority, other things keep getting in the way.

Some authors have fears about their ability to write or whether or not anyone will value what they write or buy their book. For others, the challenge is making the time to write their book or having accountability to finish it.

It's not just finding the time and confidence to write that is an obstacle. Most authors get overwhelmed with the logistics of finding an editor, finding a support team, hiring an experienced designer, and figuring out all the technicalities of writing, publishing, marketing, and launching a book. Others have actually written a book and might have even published it but did not find a way to make it profitable.

For more information on how to participate in our next Defining Moments Author Training program, visit: www.MyDefiningMoments.com. Or you can email melanie@MyDefiningMoments.com.

Other Books by Defining Moments™ Press

- *Defining Moments: Coping With the Loss of a Child* - by Melanie Warner

- *Write your Bestselling Book in 8 Weeks or Less and Make a Profit - Even if No One Has Ever Heard of You* - by Melanie Warner

- *Become Brilliant: Roadmap From Fear to Courage* – by Shiran Cohen

- *Rise, Fight, Love, Repeat: Ignite Your Morning Fire* - by Jeff Wickersham

- *Life Mapping: Decoding the Blueprint of Your Soul* - by Karen Loenser

- *Ravens and Rainbows: A Mother-Daughter Story of Grit, Courage and Love After Death* – by L. Grey and Vanessa Lynn

- *Pivot You! 6 Powerful Steps to Thriving During Uncertain Times* – by Suzanne R. Sibilla

- *A Workforce Inspired: Tools to Manage Negativity and Support a Toxic-Free Workplace* – by Dolores Neira.

- Friendship Choices:5 Great Lessons on Choosing the Right Friends- by Benedictta Apraku

- Journey of 1000 Miles: A Musher and His Huskies' Journey on the Century-Old Klondike Trails - by Hank DeBruin and Tanya McCready

www.ingramcontent.com/pod-product-compliance
Lightning Source LLC
Chambersburg PA
CBHW020446220526
45464CB00002B/882